Engineering Our World

How a Bridge Is Built

By Sam Aloian

Gareth Stevens
PUBLISHING

Please visit our website, www.garethstevens.com. For a free color catalog of all our high-quality books, call toll free 1-800-542-2595 or fax 1-877-542-2596.

Library of Congress Cataloging-in-Publication Data

Aloian, Sam, author.
 How a bridge is built / Sam Aloian.
    pages cm. — (Engineering our world)
 Includes index.
 ISBN 978-1-4824-3919-9 (pbk.)
 ISBN 978-1-4824-3920-5 (6 pack)
 ISBN 978-1-4824-3921-2 (library binding)
 1. Bridges—Design and construction—Juvenile literature. I. Title.
 TG148.A56 2016
 624.2—dc23

                              2015027616

First Edition

Published in 2016 by
Gareth Stevens Publishing
111 East 14th Street, Suite 349
New York, NY 10003

Copyright © 2016 Gareth Stevens Publishing

Designer: Samantha DeMartin
Editor: Ryan Nagelhout
Spanish Translation: Alberto Jiménez

Photo credits: Cover, p. 1 dibrova/Shutterstock.com; caption boxes stoonn/Shutterstock.com; background Jason Winter/Shutterstock.com; p. 5 (inset) JENS SCHLUETER/DDP/Getty Images; p. 5 (main) Bloomberg/Bloomberg/Getty Images; p. 7 (right) FikMik/Shutterstock.com; p. 7 (left) K13 ART/Shutterstock.com; p. 9 Roman Sotola/Shutterstock.com; p. 11 © istockphoto.com/Grigorev Vladimir; p. 13 © istockphoto.com/mrak hr; p. 15 (truss) leungchopan/Shutterstock.com; p. 15 (cantilever) Ross Strachan/Shutterstock.com; p. 15 (suspension) Songquan Deng/Shutterstock.com; p. 17 © istockphoto.com/scotto72; p. 19 Jan Miko/Shutterstock.com; p. 20 (clamp) Brian Hendricks/Shutterstock.com; p. 20 (glue) Aksenova Natalya/Shutterstock.com; p. 20 (wood craft sticks) natrot/Shutterstock.com; p. 21 (girl) Brocreative/Shutterstock.com.

Printed in the United States of America

CPSIA compliance information: Batch #CW16GS: For further information contact Gareth Stevens, New York, New York at 1-800-542-2595.

Contents

Words in the glossary appear in **bold** type the first time they are used in the text.

Place to Place

Traveling from place to place over water hasn't always been easy. Early boats were slow-moving and didn't hold many people. Oftentimes, a bridge is built to move people over water. A bridge is made of a **span** and the supports that hold it up.

There are different kinds of bridges. Some are even built over objects on land. Bridges are used to move cars, bikes, or people on foot. But bridges can often be hard to build. Let's see how it's done!

Building Blocks

There's a water bridge in Germany that moves boats over land and a river! The Magdeburg Water Bridge opened in 2003 and is 3,012 feet (918 m) long.

Magdeburg Water Bridge

Some bridges don't go over water, but let different roadways or even trains pass below.

Hold It Up

Bridges need to be able to carry lots of weight. To do this over a long period of time, they need to be **flexible** and strong. For much of history, bridges could only be made with simple **materials**. Wood and rope were often used together. These bridges were flexible, but the natural materials wore down quickly.

Some early bridges were made of stone. Stone is strong, but stone bridges are heavy and not very flexible, so they couldn't be used to make long spans.

Building Blocks

Today, steel and material called concrete are used to build most bridges. They allow bridges to stretch longer distances and carry more weight.

Engineers need to know the load, or amount of weight a bridge is holding, to figure out how to best support the **structure**.

Using the Forces

There are many different forces at work on a bridge. The load is pulled down by **gravity**, which bends materials toward Earth. This creates other forces like tension—pulling apart—and compression—squeezing together—on other bridge materials.

Different design types use these forces to their advantage. Gravity moves weight onto supports that carry a bridge's load. Beam bridges use long **horizontal** beams and vertical supports called piers. A truss bridge uses a **framework** of steel to create strong triangle shapes to support its horizontal beams.

Building Blocks

Another type of bridge—called a suspension bridge—uses cables stretched from tall towers to support the bridge's load.

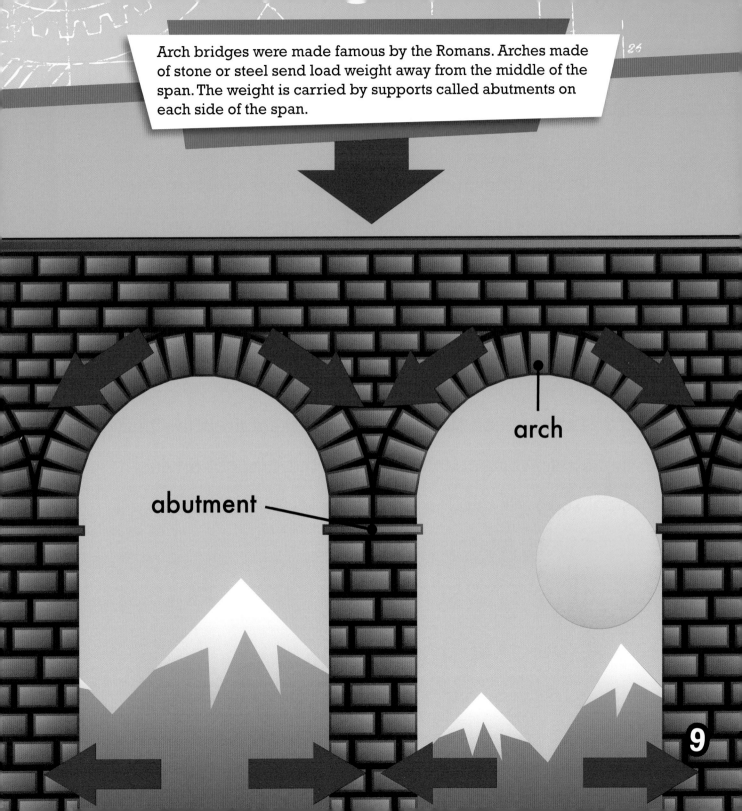

Arch bridges were made famous by the Romans. Arches made of stone or steel send load weight away from the middle of the span. The weight is carried by supports called abutments on each side of the span.

arch

abutment

Get to Work

Bridge construction starts after engineers decide what kind of bridge is needed. Beam bridges are the most common. Short beam bridges can be made quickly, while longer stretches can take years! Longer beam bridges need vertical supports in the middle of their span. These are built first with concrete and steel.

Construction starts with concrete footings for these supports. Workers drill deep into the ground, driving steel supports into the earth and laying concrete to build strong footings.

Building Blocks

Bridge supports built in the water are called piers. Engineers decide where to put piers by studying the rocks beneath the water. They need strong pier supports to carry the bridge's load.

If piers can't be built in the water, an engineer may need to use a different style of bridge to complete the job.

Falsework

Once the piers and abutments are in place, they're capped with concrete. The supports for the deck of the bridge are now built. Workers build **temporary** supports, called falsework, made of steel and wood. Falsework keeps beams and other bridge pieces in place while they're added to the structure.

Steel beams are made at a factory and shipped to the location. Giant cranes move these heavy beams into place, and workers use large bolts to link the beams together.

Building Blocks

At water level, piers are round or diamond shaped. These shapes allow water to flow around the pier more easily, reducing stress on the piers. The diamond-shaped structure is called a cutwater.

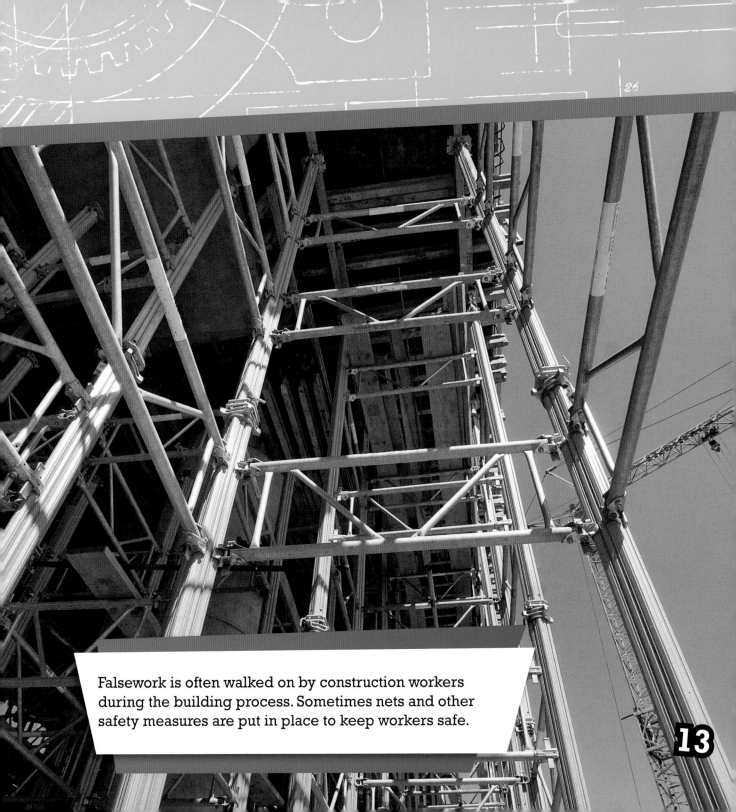

Falsework is often walked on by construction workers during the building process. Sometimes nets and other safety measures are put in place to keep workers safe.

Bridge Types

Some bridges need more steel than others to hold up, or suspend, more weight. A suspension bridge uses steel cables connected to tall towers to carry the weight of a bridge. Cantilever bridges are supported on just one end. They use trusses above and below the bridge's deck to carry weight on its piers.

Steel bridge pieces are slowly built out from supports and joined together. Some bridges need to balance their steel and falsework on both sides during construction, or the bridge could fail!

Building Blocks

Beam bridges usually aren't used to span more than 250 feet (76 m). The further apart a beam bridge's support pillars are, the weaker it is.

cantilever

suspension

truss

Some bridge trusses have amazing designs, but all the steel used is doing hard work carrying the bridge's load.

On Deck

Once the supporting steel of a bridge is in place, the decking is built. This is what the cars, trucks, and people will use to cross the bridge. Most deckings are built with large premade pieces called slabs. These slabs are made of concrete hardened around steel rods called rebar.

Some bridges, such as cantilever bridges, add the decking at the same time their structural steel is put in place. They add steel and a slab of concrete at the same time on each end to keep the structure balanced.

Building Blocks

Concrete and rebar are used together because steel can handle tensile stress—bending—while concrete handles compressive, or squeezing, stress well. This type of concrete is called **reinforced** concrete.

Adding weight on each side of the tower helps it stay balanced as the bridge's load is **distributed**.

17

Joining Together

The concrete slabs are attached to the steel structure using large bolts. Gaps between the slabs are tied together with rebar. Sometimes slabs are connected with **joints** that allow the bridge to **expand** and contract. Fresh concrete is poured in the other gaps and allowed to set. This gives the bridge a flat road surface.

Once the decking is complete, road lines are added and the bridge's steel is painted. Once engineers have tested the bridge, it's ready for use!

Building Blocks

The "life" of a bridge is the amount of time it can be safely used. Each bridge has a different life-span. Engineers constantly study bridges to make sure they're safe.

Guardrails and other fencing are also put up to make sure cars and people don't fall off the bridge!

Make Your Own Truss

Now that you know how bridges are built, try to make your own. Here's what you need to build your own truss bridge!

What You Need:

- glue

- paper and pencil

- wooden craft sticks

- clamps

How to:

1. draw truss design on paper

2. lay out popsicle sticks to match

3. glue sticks together

4. clamp sticks while drying

5. make second truss

6. connect trusses together

7. finish bridge decking

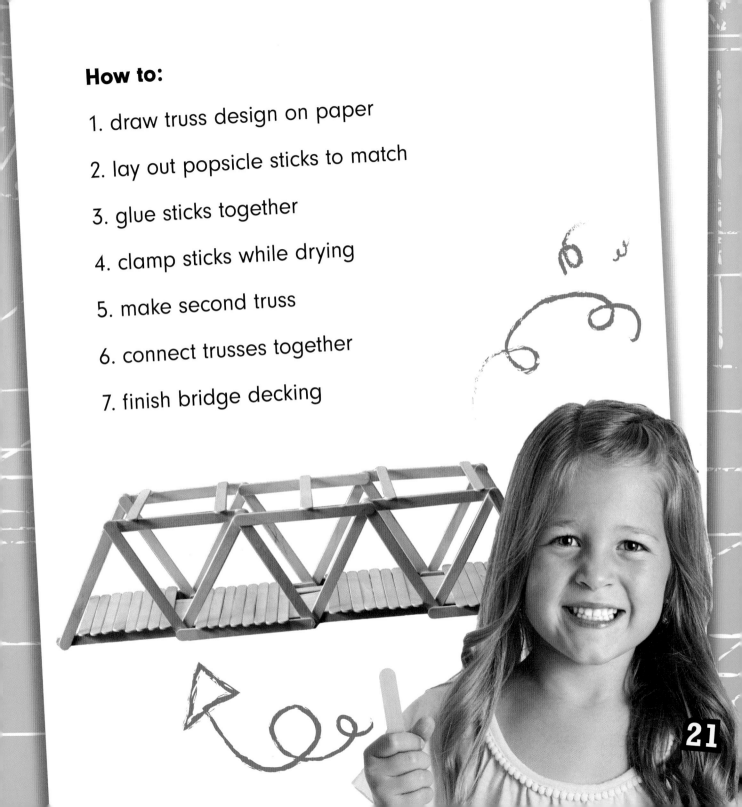

Glossary

distribute: to spread out evenly

engineer: someone who plans and builds bridges and other structures

expand: to get bigger

flexible: able to bend easily

framework: the basic supporting structure of something

gravity: the force that pulls objects toward Earth's center

horizontal: straight across from left to right

joint: a place where two things connect

material: matter that something is made of

reinforce: to make stronger by adding something

span: a spread from one support to another. Also, a length of time.

structure: the way that something is built. Also, something that is built by putting parts together and that usually stands on its own.

temporary: lasting for a short time

For More Information

Books

Carmichael, L. E. *Amazing Feats of Civil Engineering*. Minneapolis, MN: Essential Library, 2015.

Hoena, Blake. *Building the Golden Gate Bridge: An Interactive Engineering Adventure*. North Mankato, MN: Capstone Press, 2015.

Stefoff, Rebecca. *Building Bridges*. New York, NY: Cavendish Square Publishing, 2016.

Websites

Bridge Basics
pghbridges.com/basics.htm
This site shows the many different kinds of bridges that engineers build.

Five Bridge Types
www.aiacincinnati.org/community/abc/curriculum/fivebridgetypes.pdf
See how the forces of load, tension, and compression work on different types of bridges here.

Index